SOUND OF T

D0861309

PITT POETRY SERIES
Ed Ochester, Editor

SOUND OF THE AX

Aphorisms and Poems

by William Stafford

Edited by Vincent Wixon and Paul Merchant

UNIVERSITY OF PITTSBURGH PRESS

Published by the University of Pittsburgh Press, Pittsburgh, Pa., 15260
Copyright © 2014, The Estate of William Stafford
All rights reserved
Manufactured in the United States of America
Printed on acid-free paper
10 9 8 7 6 5 4 3 2 1
ISBN 13: 978-0-8229-6296-0
ISBN 10: 0-8229-6296-9

In memory of
Dorothy Hope Stafford
1916–2013

Editors' Preface

An aphorism is a metaphor in work clothes, the kind of statement that "delivers groceries," as William Stafford put it. This volume includes nearly four hundred of the thousands of aphoristic statements that occur at regular intervals throughout William Stafford's fifty years of daily writing. It was part of William Stafford's writing practice to create or, as he might say, "discover" aphorisms; often one will appear on the same journal page as a description of a dream and drafts of a poem. Or they might appear in bunches, as when Stafford mused over a number of days about what the wind might say, out of which he chose twelve statements to arrange for his poem "Things the Wind Says." As befits his wide-ranging mind, Stafford's aphorisms explore a multitude of topics, such as faith and harmony, the lives of animals, art and writing, how to behave, war and peace, loyalty, appearance and reality, history, honesty, egoism, work, fears, all expressed in a concise, witty, and provocative way.

In poems, aphorisms can open doors ("A thing of beauty is a joy forever."), take stock ("I have measured out my life with coffee spoons."), or mark a terminus ("Good fences make good neighbors."). A characteristic aspect of William Stafford's poetry is the aphoristic line that perfectly encapsulates the thought of a whole poem: "The bitter habit of the forlorn cause / is my addiction." "We live in an occupied country, misunderstood; / justice will take us millions of intricate moves." "What the river says, that is what I say."

William Stafford delighted in occasionally creating whole poems from fragments of wisdom: what he thought of as "list poems." In an interview he called such poems "just a succession of things the way the world gives you things . . . an aggregation of things to say," as in the well-known "Things I Learned Last Week" or "The Sparkle Depends on Flaws in the Diamond," in which even the title is an aphorism. More frequently, in other poems, such as "Butterflies in the Radiator Grill" or "Optimism," aphorisms work with other poetic elements to achieve a meaning often surprising but conclusive. This volume collects twenty-six poems written between 1949 and 1993.

There are a number of inspirations for the aphoristic tendency in William Stafford's writing. We know from Stafford's late-published essay "Sometimes, Reading" that his discovery at the University of Kansas of Nietzsche's *The Birth of Tragedy* introduced him to "a changed world, deeper but full of wonder." And in the accompanying list of his early reading we find other aphoristic authors, some mentioned in this volume: Pascal and Kierkegaard, each a lifetime mentor. But Nietzsche's "blazes of outrageous but tantalizing discovery" take first place in his attention. He quotes three of Nietzsche's phrases, "Every word is a prejudice," "The best way through the mountains is from peak to peak, but it takes long legs," "The right eye shouldn't trust the left," any of which, in their sharpness and surprising shape, could be a Stafford aphorism.

Other sources include the sayings of Heraclitus, the essays of Montaigne, William Blake's "Proverbs of Hell," the ghazals of Ghalib (Stafford's most brilliant foray into translation), and the inspired voices of Augustine of Hippo, Teresa of Avila, and Gandhi. Finally, there is Carl Sandburg's *The People, Yes*, published in 1936, from which Stafford quoted in a piece written during the last month of his life. In his trenchant review of Carolyn Forché's *Against Forgetting: Twentieth Century Poetry of Witness*, Stafford comments that "Carl Sandburg mentions somewhere the value of having 'a good forgettery.'" Sandburg's book, a lively mixture of prose aphorisms and terse poems, is filled with familiar lines: "Somewhere they'll give a war and nobody will come"; "You can fool all of the people part of the time and part of the people all of the time, but you can't fool all of the people all of the time"; "'There ain't no strong coffee, only weak people,' said one heavy on the java." These examples give some sense of the volume's sardonic wisdom and would explain the pleasing irony that a book Stafford likely read in the early 1940s provided the phrase "a good forgettery" fifty years later.

Like Pascal, Blake, Ghalib, and his fellow Midwesterner Sandburg, William Stafford knew the value of brevity and wit when communicating truths, especially inconvenient ones. His practice of this art became a lifetime of gradually accumulating "things to say" that we have come to regard as his authentic voice. This voice, a solace to many readers, and an inspiration or goad to many others, allowed him to speak truth to power from his days as a conscientious objector during the Second World War to his last great poems of wartime protest in the early 1990s. It is a quiet voice, and often very funny, but these small utterances characteristically enter the mind with a jolt of revelation.

Vincent Wixon and Paul Merchant

SOUND OF THE AX

Of this world, I am a little part reaching outward.

When he saw the leopard jump, he knew he was poor.

All events and experiences are local, somewhere.

When the snake decided to go straight he didn't get anywhere.

Lost pioneers were the ones who found the best valleys.

It still takes all kinds to make a world, but there's an oversupply of some.

It is legitimate to crawl, after the wings are broken.

There are many of those who have sense enough to come in out of the rain who do not have sense enough to go out in the sun.

Many things true when said, the world makes
untrue.

Every mink has a mink coat.

Off a high place, it is courtesy to let others go first.

The wars we haven't had saved many lives.

What the locomotive says, the whole train does.

By bending, the grass develops a surface.

No ditch without its willow.

Climbing along the River

Willows never forget how it feels
to be young.

Do you remember where you came from?
Gravel remembers.

Even the upper end of the river
believes in the ocean.

Exactly at midnight
yesterday sighs away.

What I believe is,
all animals have one soul.

Over the land they love
they crisscross forever.

The real artist's life is a work of art.

In Oregon the coyotes are still the best poets.

Trees do not demand any response, whatever their stance.

When a whale gets away, you're willing to range far to find it.

Birds are a hope: they can find the islands left.

The jaguar at the dance; a silken leash.

His trouble is that he has lived according to principles instead of according to how he feels. (Now he doesn't know how he feels.)

Our "intelligence" is just our luck—our happening to experience things in the right order to make us in harmony with the needs we face.

I don't want to do anything *to be an example* to anyone.

All errors are errors of taste.

I must see farther, even when no one says, "Look!"

To hold the voice down and the eyes up when facing someone who antagonizes you is a slight weight— once. But in a lifetime it adds up to tons.

Moss remembers the rain.

The root and the flower have to trust each other.

The Sparkle Depends on Flaws in the Diamond

Wood that can learn is no good for a bow.

The eye that can stand the sun can't
   see in shadow.

Fish don't find the channel—the channel
   finds them.

If the root doesn't trust, the plant
   won't blossom.

A dog that knows jaguars is no longer
   useful in hunting.

You can lie at a banquet, but you have to
   be honest in the kitchen.

The grace we need to find will not be found by the graceful only.

A realization: my slogan for writing—lower your standards and go on—applies to living, to getting old.

So light the bird, so heavy the mountain.

Being a wild duck takes a lot of flying.

Every person should save a part of each day—at least a half-hour, and an hour would be better—for what could be labeled just looking out the window; that is, a time for turning away from immediate outer demands that wear away the self.

I belong to so many minority groups.

The *revolution* is the opiate of some of the people.

Solid veneer.

The kind of falling that may mean learning to walk.

I imagine a perfect sensibility that pours completely
into each experience along the way. A sentence
becomes a whole boiling millrace.

She likes animals because they can do without blame
what people can do only at the cost of guilt.

We are a school of fish in a lake. Nobody signals,
but when we all begin to turn, everyone adjusts. We
think the world is the shape of our lake.

It's *all right*—this is what I wanted to tell the young.

Before you hear the music, you do the dance.

Keepsakes

Star Guides:
    Any star is enough
    if you know what star it is.

Kids:
    They dance before they learn
    there is anything that isn't music.

The Limbs of the Pin Oak Tree:
    "Gravity—what's that?"

An Argument Against the Empirical Method:
    Some haystacks don't even have any needle.

Comfort:
    We think it is calm here,
    or that our storm is the right size.

How shall the lion feed if the deer be saved?

It's the dirt makes a garden.

A good workman will trust—and at the same time suspect—his tools.

Enticed by knowledge we have gone forward, proudly, farther into the lion's mouth.

As Frankenstein found out, sometimes you succeed in a project and find you've created a monster.

Everything I say coils inward toward what I have to say. No matter how I want to lie.

The wider your knowledge, the milder your opinions?

It's ridiculous but the old begin to be proud of their age.

My tremors are small, perhaps unmeaning, but like
Galileo I can go away muttering, "Still, it moves."

I would honor the world in some common way but my
way to be common is my own.

Trouble with explaining about poetry: The words
are always carrying on a clandestine affair with each
other, and implicating the thought.

To be happy only with unattainable things.

Grace: the accepting of one or the other of an either-or
choice.

I write short things because no one will listen long.

I follow a trail the hounds lost years ago.

Note

straw, feathers, dust—
little things

but if they all go one way,
that's the way the wind goes.

People should help their kids know decisively which way is north, if they know which way north is.

Mornings, I have spells of desire to tell the truth.

When you write, what you ignore is absent, but what you deny is present.

It was in corners of our selves that the world was falling down.

Successful people are in a rut.

The astounding, continuing variety of routine. It is far too much for me to take in.

Aggressive people do not appeal to me; I yield them scorched earth.

Those who champion democracy, but also make a fetish of never accepting anything they don't agree with—what advantage do they see in democracy?

I do not want to become good in any way but my own way.

Believing our way, we find.

People who serve pancakes are always trying to pretty them up—orange juice, applesauce, etc.; but the charm of pancakes is that they are just pancakes.

If I stayed true to all my earlier loyalties I'd be overwhelmed right now: we survive by forgetting.

Every mountain has that one place when you begin to know it is a mountain.

The Sun is thousands of times bigger than Earth; I block it out with my hand.

Even if you're blind, there is still light.

Sayings of the Blind

Feeling is believing.

Mountains don't exist. But their slopes do.

Little people have low voices.

All things, even the rocks, make a little noise.

The silence back of all sound is called "the sky."

There's a big stranger in town called the sun.
    He doesn't speak to us but puts out a hand.

Night opens a door into a cellar—
    you can smell it coming.

On Sundays everyone stands farther apart.

Velvet feels black.

Meeting cement is never easy.

What do they mean when they say night is gloomy?

Edison didn't invent much.

Whenever you wake up it's morning.

Names have a flavor.

The arrow tells what the archer meant to say.

Bright lights create sharp shadows.

Some kinds of integrity are excuses for irresponsibility.

I am not guided in my political choices by a calculation
of what others will choose. Ask me what I want and
I'll tell you.

No one can avoid prejudice—personality is prejudice,
character is prejudice, identity is prejudice. The issue
is, which prejudices you have.

The cost of epics may ruin all this world.

Writing isn't thoughts, or principles, or character—
it's words. It's words with a life of their own. And the
writer—though suspicious of that life, and not in
control of it—is impressed and somehow hopeful: he
strings along.

Yes, I've been thinking quite a bit recently. But there are still quite a few things I haven't thought of yet.

If it happens to me, it's all right.

When all you are trying to do is the right thing, it isn't hard to act, for you have no distractions.

What can't be avoided must be endured.

War is in the soldier. He dies when it starts.

Why should an anthropologist quarrel with the customs he goes to study?

Just story—taste of story—is enough to stir me, no matter the content.

Sayings from the Northern Ice

It is people at the edge who say
things at the edge: winter is toward knowing.

    Sled runners before they meet have long talk apart.
    There is a pup in every litter the wolves will have.
    A knife that falls points at an enemy.
    Rocks in the wind know their place: down low.
    Over your shoulder is God; the dying deer sees Him.

At the mouth of the long sack we fall in forever
storms brighten the spikes of the stars.

    Wind that buried bear skulls north of here
    and beats moth wings for help outside the door
    is bringing bear skull wisdom, but do not ask the skull
    too large a question till summer.
    Something too dark was held in that strong bone.

Better to end with a lucky saying:

    Sled runners cannot decide to join or to part.
    When they decide, it is a bad day.

Our best work derives merely from a continuity of our daily selves.

Art is first nothing, then something.

Planting trees is *hedging* with time: you want it to pass so the trees will be big.

The heroes of the landscape: hills, blue jays, the kind of weed that grows where the river flooded, a lost dog finding a trail—certainly no person. My mind blows about like dandelion seed.

Working with cement—it has a lot of forgive. It has a terrific clench when it mixes with steel.

Sometimes maybe we need to do what we intended to do, because we intended to do it.

I'd just as soon be in favor of things that happen.

Maybe we're just worms, but we eat the mulberry leaves of experience and turn them into silk.

A place became a door because there was a next place.

Entering a book is letting a book change you.

Anyway, history has me in it.

It is a temptation to try to be good at your job.

For a while the sun can be our guide, then the remembered moon, and then the coming of another kind of light.

Though we often turned we never wandered.

Butterflies in the Radiator Grill

Arrayed like Solomon, the radiator grill
snores into itself blue, brown, yellow, gray—
all the colors that the flowers of the field
in their innocence, their carelessness, betray.

Lives we pass, a screen takes us.
There are lines we cross like warnings on our way,
so cruel that summer sings out. Storms,
we all travel toward one big storm some day.

Before you have your dreams, your dreams have
you, and every day pushes a night before it while the
wilderness follows.

All you listen for is sound.

My behavior, voices, appearance, talk—observed and
reported precisely—would to certain people have a
steady effect of irony.

I don't like to delete and focus—but to grasp:
paintings make me desperate to get out of the frame.

Because I was caught where his hate flowed, he had
to lavish too rich an emotion for me.

Now is made out of ghosts.

Come, be human. Sit down and let's talk.

Most people say stories embody ideas, religious, and other thought patterns already formed; but actually we learn religions and ideas from stories.

Faith is easy; doubt is hard.

Often you do the right thing but the wrong thing still happens.

Even to know whether you have made a mistake is to know—to be smarter than when you first acted.

It takes time and luck to make an experiment or a poem.

The great worth of a place; it reared the people who rejected it.

To say someone has "run out of material" for writing is to use a metaphor. He is not a container of material.

Written on the Stub of the First Paycheck

Gasoline makes game scarce.
In Elko, Nevada, I remember a stuffed wildcat
someone had shot on Bing Crosby's ranch.
I stood in the filling station
breathing fumes and reading the snarl of a map.

There were peaks to the left so high
they almost got away in the heat;
Reno and Las Vegas were ahead.
I had promise of the California job,
and three kids with me.

It takes a lot of miles to equal one wildcat
today. We moved into a housing tract.
Every dodging animal carries my hope in Nevada.
It has been a long day, Bing.
Wherever I go is your ranch.

My typical act is—hit the road.

We put in a cottonwood post. It rooted and leafed.

What if you could stun everyone into having the
same good dream: that's what a literary work
accomplishes, momentarily.

One trouble about language is that people sometimes
believe what you say, and you were only trying it out.

Maybe a need has made me "intellectual":—the need
to turn like a terrier on any assertion, and worry it
till it comes level with all the context I can find.

There is such a thing as helping history to get along
with its dirty work.

Never point a truth at someone unless it is good for
him—or you intend to shoot him with it.

I found in the clutter at the workbench my cup, the coffee just cool enough to drink.

Rabbits when they jump own for a moment the whole disregarded universe.

Being right is manifesting enough originality for me.

Every day when I write I feel I'm getting to the main business of my soul.

All the hounds came back with a better bite.

I have honor, but little profit, in my own country.

The way I predict is, I wait to see what happens.

Why shouldn't poems tell you things you need to know?

Song Now

Guitar string is.
Everything else can wait.
Silence puts a paw
wherever the music rests.

All we have is need.
Before and After are falling.
Now is going away.
Sound is the only sky.

Guitar string is:
it can save this place.

There might be someone so successful you wouldn't know it.

Beat your megaphones into ear trumpets.

When you fear winter, summer is over.

Fiction: Events occur with built-in justifications and justifying accompaniments: Achilles laments *by the sea;* Odysseus wavers *before the wind;* Don Quixote thinks *in a cracked helmet;* Aeneas founds a city, *carrying fragments of one;* Robinson Crusoe is alone *on an island,* etc.

The shorter the candle, the longer the shadow.

Arrows punish a bow.

I no longer yearn to explain, or to find out details, to justify, to try out alternatives, in the course of past events. The river that passed our house has long ago reached the sea.

If there is a trail, you have taken a wrong turn.

A famous man came to us, buried under his name.
When we said it, grazing horses raised their heads.

I think of the people who tell me they have to write
because they have so much to tell the world. I write
not because I understand and want to expose, but
because I understand nothing. I experience newness
every day and write of it as the first tasting of interest.

So a sentence won't drain away, you put a period at
the end of it.

The fault of one foot is the opportunity of the other.

The past relax, the future tense.

Somewhere deep where we have no program—our
next discovery lies.

Where there is no directive all ways are equally good.
The river always finds the right way, if there is a way.

Wild Horse Lore

Downhill, any gait will serve.

It tastes good—a little snow
    on old hay.

A stylish mane finds
    the wind.

The world, and enough grass—
    we don't need the cavalry
    any more.

Where I walk is road, but where I look around is wilderness, if I look far enough.

In a rich country the good life consists not in "and" but "or."

You are inside the story, telling it, even when you think you are outside.

Poetry does not state; it manifests.

My kind of faith is that most mountains won't move.

In small things a person could be exemplary while perhaps in one large thing absolutely to be condemned.

My life isn't what I thought it was. But the world isn't either.

Mean people: They have to think a certain way to be like that—the quality of their lives is their punishment.

Alone. Remember. Fear. Not three words: three worlds.

The world is what you see outside your window plus what you think of.

I hate those gifts when it's the thought behind it.

I distrust language and the treachery I feel in it.

The truth is, every day brings a different possibility—and a doubt about yesterday.

A gun can choose. A bullet has no choice.

Truth has no perspective.

.38

This metal has come to look at
your eye. Look at its eye—that
stare that can't lose.

There's no grin like a gun—
as if only its calm
could soothe your hand.

But metal is cold,
cold. In the night, in the risk,
it's a touch of the dead.

It's a cold world.

The sky is bigger than any country.

Bad opinions drive out good.

If you hate other people, you are rejecting qualities
you have yourself.

Citizens feel they represent their country, that they
identify with what it does. The individual, though, is
riding a tiger. To guide one's country is like guiding
a tornado.

By the sound a pen makes you can't tell where it is
going.

A poem knows where you already are, and it nails
you there.

The language of religion is divisive partly because it
tries to state what cannot be stated.

Once you learn to trust your sensation of being lost,
you are found. The *other* end of the compass needle
is just as reliable as the north end.

Everything has meaning. Be a total receiver.

Sentences are symptoms, including this one.

If you stay balanced, successive things you say can
have an exquisite shimmer, a promise that stays alive
like a harmony in music.

Forced language reveals its forcing.

An owl needs dark to see.

A scholar applies a rule; an artist follows a lead.

The three hundred acre meadow has a headlong,
silent stream, grass, mushrooms, trees, birds,
badgers, coyotes. It *balances* in the evening.

The Gospel Is Whatever Happens

When we say, "Breath,"
a feather starts to fly,
to be itself.
When we talk, truth
is what we mean to say.

A weather vane is
courteous and accurate:
the more it yields,
the more wind lies
where it points the way.

If you will grant me one vivid morning, I can chain it to me for fifty years.

Children are near death—they remember it, they have just come from it. They look around at a world new. The old have forgotten. The world is theirs, life is a habit, they have had it long.

The point of view creates the emotion and value, in any narrative—"See that one poor lion that doesn't have any Christian."

To admire, one has to be limited enough.

Anyone very old talking about the danger and violence of the world is a walking contradiction: there would be no survivors in the scene many people depict.

The golden bough grows from your hand.

Pascal said eloquence is vanity.

Can you be honest and not tell the truth? Yes—
because you may not know the truth.

What I put in rhymes with something I didn't put in.

My dreams are quick, like fish. They number through
my recent days, not intense, not extreme, just fast and
changing, as if I must tell over and over again all
recent events till they have no shadow.

Those who say Emily Dickinson lived a dull life . . .

In a cold light the black doors of the locomotive wait.
When I see it, the fire inside it flares. I have a place
for anything offered—anything that meets me lives.

It is snowing what I will know. And it is melting what
I will forget.

I am sociable because my poems are about lonely things.

So Long

At least at night, a streetlight
is better than a star.
And better good shoes on a
long walk, than a good friend.

Often in winter with my old
cap I slip away into the gloom
like a happy fish, at home
with all I touch, at the level of love.

No one can surface till far,
far on, and all that we'll have
to love may be what's near
in the cold, even then.

"In wildness is the preservation of the world." I say try to be tame; try to deny the lively turns of your thought: it lives wild anyway.

Someone said language was invented so we could hide our thoughts. By now my thoughts are undiscoverable. Maybe silence would build character again.

Getting older, you learn things—like *why* the old take little steps, *why* they move more slowly. And you learn something about the young: that your presence and participation in the world is not that important, and neither is theirs.

Literature is words that merit being said *again*.

If we are to have great poets, we must have audiences stupid enough—or brilliant enough—to follow with sympathy what a poem says.

Anything said implies the kind of speaker who would say that.

The things you do not have to say make you rich. Saying things you do not have to say weakens your talk. Hearing things you do not need to hear dulls your hearing. And things you know before you hear them— those are you, those are why you are in the world.

Creative writing is like doing a journey in which the traveling creates the goal.

Prizes won't save your soul.

Talking about poetry is like talking about love—it's a long way from doing it.

A rejection slip: "This is too good for our readers."

If you count the leaves every day you will not grow many trees.

Sinner that I am, couldn't I cast even a little stone?

No one has to tell you when a skunk arrives.

Many things we think we are leaving are waiting for us.

Salvaged Parts

Fire took the house. Black bricks
tell how it went. Wild roses
try to say it never happened.

A rock my foot pushed falls
for years down the cellar stairs. . . .
No thanks, no home again for me—

Mine burned before it burned.
A rose pretends, but I always knew:
a rose pretends, a rock tells how it is.

Only by sending roots deep does the treetop avoid the ground.

A speech is something you say so as to distract attention from what you do not say.

It is disquieting to teach, or lecture. I want to be in the back row again.

I've got in a lot of trouble in my life by being careful.

Time has separated into events. Between them time rests. Moments of the wind, then nothing. The world leans against the door, and the latch moves.

The world is an old place. Everything has already happened once.

Surrealism relates to the little hump of help attention needs toward perceiving the less than obvious.

Writing must learn to be as easy as talk.

Rocks that fail become sand.

The world has great power to preserve itself—it still squeezes people between the mountains and the sea.

Poetry is the kind of thing you have to see from the corner of your eye. You can be too well prepared for poetry. A conscientious interest in it is worse than no interest at all. If you analyze it away, it's gone. It would be like boiling a watch to find out what makes it tick.

The arts maintain the life that realizes while it is lived.

Treat the world as if it really existed.

Please don't turn the windmill off even at night when it creaks or the tank is full—there are some flowers by the overflow pipe.

Artist, Come Home

Remember how bright it is,
the old rabbitbush by the hall light?

One of the blackberry vines has
reached all the way to the clothesline.

There isn't any way to keep
the kitchen window from tapping.

The tea kettle had one of its meditative
spells yesterday.

I am thinking again of that old
plan—breakfast first, then the newspaper.

They say maybe they won't have
that big war this year after all.

A frog is living under the
back step.

The world is a long poem I am falling through—I just tell about it.

Many critics treat a novel or poem as a statement. But it is better considered as a performance.

We must not admire the world—a nerve pinches, or something else goes wrong in us, and the world is worthless.

No dreams but the one: "reality."

In the shell where I was living they told me to come out—they had a bigger shell.

You are part of what you criticize, or you don't know enough about it to criticize.

Oregon is insanely green. It is the thin light left over from Eden.

A wilderness is something in the mind. I live there. I walk around in its great big footprint. I want to hold those prints in the light. Years later of course the trail is gone.

Any chunk of carbon under pressure will turn into a diamond.

Lonely as the universe is, that's where I live, and it is where all my education has been preparing me to live.

In writing, a trick is to give yourself good assignments.

We live in language as a sea creature lives, drawing from our surroundings millions of nourishments, all naturally, without necessarily being conscious of that nourishment.

Other parts of the car can say maybe, but the battery has to say yes.

Water is always ready to learn.

Things the Wind Says

Everything still ought to move.

Of all plants I believe my favorite
    is the tumbleweed.

Water will talk if stirred.

There are places in the mountains I am
    afraid to tell about, but at night
    you can hear me hint about them.

Islands aren't so much.

I never saw a cloud I didn't like.

Steam is all right, but I prefer smoke.

I was born in Kansas, but now I
    travel all over the world.

I spend my vacations in Texas.

The best job I ever had was with
    Sir Francis Drake.

My cousins live in water: they're a
    slow bunch.

I'll dance with anyone—royalty, commoners,
    but especially refugees. . . .

A fierce walking—to see, hear, smell, taste, feel something. This takes the place of a vocation.

Does life have a plot? At first I thought a person might impose some untrue pattern, myth, on experience so that the belief would make living easier, better. Then I thought: everyone does.

I want to know fewer things but know them more.

The ideal teacher—someone who can't talk.

Choose a villain. Hitler, say. Our feelings about him are a result of his actions. What were his feelings a result of?

When you rebel against human activities and values, you are not leaving human activities and values behind.

You can compost newspapers.

Poetry is prose without the mistakes.

Seeing the work of Dutch painters—the gesture of making something from whatever is there.

Writing comes about through quick, successive, cumulative overlays of opportunity put upon any chance beginning.

I will follow my experiments, even if they don't converge with needs.

"I'm wrong about that."—one of the handy sentences.

If people notice and commend you, are those the things you should do?

"What they don't know won't hurt them."—then what they know may hurt them? Then elective ignorance is helpful?

Optimism

What you can make with a knife
you can mar with a knife. Lift
this one; look far ahead—
many whittled sticks, apples
quartered, a stab or two,
maybe a death. Heft it.

Why go on? Why
suffer? Well, the blade,
the fine, smooth curve of it;
and then—you know—the apples.

Rich in what I forget.

Is that a clock, or a bomb, ticking?

Some writers keep us disquieted; the central quality
of their work seems to be that stretch between
understanding and not understanding. Surreal,
existential, mystic, Zen, etc.—they all keep the bait
ahead of us.

It is a tall order, finding your way. Maybe it's winter
and you can't just stand around waiting for help.

There are thought clichés, and no degree of care with
language can hide that lack of quality.

Are there any differences among people? Yes. Then
even in enemy nations there are differences in how
firm the "enemy" feelings are? Yes. Does this make
any difference in your reactions? Well. . . .

Save the world by torturing one innocent child?
What innocent child?

Being wrong is easy. *How* to be when wrong is harder.

For now, here are the rules: Be someone. Be here.

You give up something for everything you get, but because your attention is on what you get you don't notice. The gain is noticed; the loss may become noticeable later.

Defer or else. The "or else" part is a career.

I went into the cabin and closed the door against the wilderness, but all night it was still there.

Talk and writing are to me not messages, not expressions, not communications, but are *evidence*.

The common sense view of life is untenable.

You can hear better if it's dark.

Buddha's Thoughts

In a mountain that is one big stone
a crack is considering:
we are saved by that hesitation.

All trees lean in the spring
but soon toughen for winter
waiting to say the great name.

In this world, what I really like
are these things that don't happen.

A river that had one bank was lost.

For People Who Wonder at What I Write: Sometimes the paper moves; I just hold my pen.

Go in peace—but go.

The trouble with the news is—it's usually about people.

On the citation for fame and excellence they misspelled my name.

Chance forms you. Chance preserves you. Chance will destroy you.

Joseph Conrad and the *sea*. Van Gogh and the *sun*. Henry James and the *talk*. Willa Cather and *civilization*. Shakespeare and *decision*.

About the pessimists: how can they know that much?

Deciding to be objective is a subjective decision.

You don't really have to please anybody.

For me, revision is making it wilder, not tamer.

Poems are expendable, but the process is not expendable; it is lifelong.

Sometimes what I write scares me.

Which side of the gate are the locks on?

The idea of choosing some fake compass and relying absolutely on it is untenable.

Put These in Your Pipe

In a crash my head hit the pavement—
I've had the world in me ever since.

The doctor listens to my heart—
yes, I know what time it is.

I walk out and stand in a clearing
while the snow falls all around.

Children, that country you cry about,
that's where we all have to live.

Whenever the worst times came
doves have shared my sorrow.

Wherever God has sent me,
the meadowlarks were already there.

I think of something to end with,
but I'm not going to write it down.

Sometimes you leave the tools in, after the operation.

Like a frog at a moonrise, I am impressed but not reverent.

To know all is to forgive nothing.

If I resent someone's arrogance, is it because I have that competitive quality from which arrogance comes?

Winners can lose what winning was for.

Some questions you would ask of God prove you unfit for God's company.

If my enemies are strong and right, are they enemies? And if they are mistaken, should I work to help them?

Between roars the lion purrs.

To call some people losers is to reveal your limits in defining categories into which people can go.

The genius we ascribe to others is a return on the expectations we feel smart enough to have.

A Response for Those Who Told Us How Dumb We Were: You think we didn't know?

It gets old, being young all the time.

I hoped they would save that oak east of the prison.

What a person is shows up in what a person does.

If you live long enough, serious things will happen.

Consolations

"The broken part heals even stronger than the rest,"
they say. But that takes awhile.
And, "Hurry up," the whole world says.
They tap their feet. And it still hurts on rainy
afternoons when the same absent sun
gives no sign it will ever come back.

"What difference in a hundred years?"
The barn where Agnes hanged her child
will fall by then, and the scrawled words
erase themselves on the floor where rats' feet
run. Boards curl up. Whole new trees
drink what the rivers bring. Things die.

"No good thing is easy." They told us that,
while we dug our fingers into the stones
and looked beseechingly into their eyes.
They say the hurt is good for you. It makes
what comes later a gift all the more
precious in your bleeding hands.

When it's your own pain, you notice it.

The river keeps looking for the perfect stone.

A common sin: Insufficient care in avoiding the
approval of others.

Other people's rights interest me because other people
are more interesting when they have their rights. If the
contrary were true, I'm afraid I'd want to deny their
rights in order to make them more interesting.

Do I respect others to the degree that I fear them?

Leaves have no politics. Each one votes with its life. All
win. And lose. Their tree descends, too, finally, with them.

This evening I learned I have been doing a ridiculous
thing: there is an old spoon in the kitchen drawer which
I don't like, and I have been giving it its *fair share* of use.

Language is my friend. I feel the language the same way a
fish feels water.

Maybe our needs are deeper than our appetites.

You can be drowning and like it if the water is warm and soothing and people keep cheering and hugging each other and waving little flags.

Some people want the world to have meanings; and some just want it to work.

Intentions have side effects.

A writer works a long time on a story, a poem; then a critic immediately sees just where the writer has gone wrong. Wouldn't it be better if the critic just wrote the story or poem in the first place?

In the war some of the enemy didn't fight very hard, and some of us didn't either. Between battles unregarded peace crept in while warriors were sleeping.

When people talk I tend to follow the words, but I should become more aware of the *tune*.

The Dream of Now

When you wake to the dream of now
from night and its other dream,
you carry day out of the dark
like a flame.

When spring comes north, and flowers
unfold from earth and its even sleep,
you lift summer on with your breath
lest it be lost ever so deep.

Your life you live by the light you find
and follow it on as well as you can,
carrying through darkness wherever you go
your one little fire that will start again.

I dreamed last night what sleep was for but now I wake.

Imagine as far as you can. A feeling that comes is religious. Imagine you carry that feeling—you are now a missionary.

If you can say it, it begins to exist.

What you can do is all right. And sometimes you get lucky.

Zen—it doesn't make sense, but I understand it.

We are surrounded, not by emblems, by paragons or villains, or fragments from Heaven and Hell, but by ready and adjustable potentials: nothing is special, everything is maybe.

I wish more of my friends said "and" rather than "but."

Kindness is my kind of aggression.

Some of the impulses and actions we regret result from qualities we have to possess in order to live.

For one generation we remember our parents, and they theirs, overlapping all the way back to somewhere. Mine have no current informant but me, and their time on earth will drop away while mine will drift and fade in my children's thought.

Recant whenever you can.

I live in a foreign country.

My aim is not to be a writer, but to write.

The sun does not judge the leaves.

Nietzsche says of someone, "He writes too loud."

Influential Writers

Some of them write too loud.

Some write the mauve poem
over and over.

In our time a whole tribe have
campaigned with noisy boots on—
they look swashbuckling but
all the syllables finally run and hide.

Their swagger makes them feel good,
but mobilizes opposition.

Listen—after a torrent begins even big rocks
have to get out of the way,
but at the top of the divide you can change
Mississippi to Columbia with one finger,
and I did.

But I didn't want the Pacific this big.

The stream is always revising.

All of us writers get up and report on which part of the elephant we touch.

My voice apparently has a tone imperceptible for some people's ears. I'm a dog sending off vibrations of the wrong frequency.

Talk has many tunes. Praise is one of the tinniest.

You had your wound—now the healing starts. The wounding is clean but the healing hurts.

Mistakes you make are guides for where to go; snowflakes the storm brings are shelter from its cold.

It wasn't that we failed, but we didn't succeed.

Playing the game: be careful to play by the real rules, not the ostensible rules—or be ready to lose.

For happiness we need our sorrows.

"Drink from your own well," Kierkegaard says.

I'd like to haunt the edges of our language, pretending to translate from languages not yet invented.

Having said something makes it possible to say something else.

After a verbal attack you turn to the attacker: "What other symptoms do you have?"

Experience mourns, but even while doing so—plans.

Mein Kampf

In those reaches of the night when your thoughts
burrow in, or at some stabbed interval
pinned by a recollection in daylight,
a better self begs its hands out to you:

That bitter tracery your life wove
looms forth, and the jagged times haggle
and excruciate your reaching palms again—
"A dull knife hurts most."

Old mistakes come calling: no life
happens just once. Whatever snags
even the edge of your days will abide.
You are a turtle with all the years on your back.

Your head sinks down into the mud.
You must bear it. You need a thick shell in that rain.

You hope. But you know.

You may win a war you are sorry to have started.

On a battlefield the flies don't care who wins.

Why should I worry? I have pens and plenty of paper.

A word is a possibility for meaning, but misleading is one of its lurking riches.

Fool that I am, I keep thinking things will work out, that we can coast along while injustice prevails, and somehow it will change.

You can make a living by championing the obvious.

Far things are romantic.

My attitude is this: where you live is not crucial, but how you *feel* about where you live is crucial.

As you know, my poems are organically grown.

I am the kind of person who wears the kind of hat I wear.

It's a constant struggle for a human being to attain anything close to the dignity and cleanness of a rock or a piece of wood.

In that war we persuaded ourselves that the people we were killing were really bad.

A new page always makes me feel optimistic.

[A Well-Oiled Gate]

A well-oiled gate won't give you a song.

Hold your glass right side up if you want a drink.

Any trouble, an oyster builds a pearl around it.

Hiring a media voice: bring your sound of honesty;
    we'll tell you what to say.

Wisdom is too heavy for the young.

Any sound that we give our lives to turns to music.

A passage you lend your life to turns into poetry.

To save myself in the snowstorm after my release, the
only thing I had to start a fire with was my pardon.

A bridge that breaks is worse than no bridge at all.

"Do you get writer's block?" "No, but maybe I
should."

On El Greco's forehead I set my coffee cup and
thought of the great and their use to us.

Writing my autobiography, I began not to like the
way it looked, and I had an impulse to revise—not
my writing, but my life: "You must revise your life!"

I say craft eats innocence.

By following his needs, Cervantes invented the novel.
And so for all: emergence is a part of emergency.

Prejudice is the wrong ideas others have about you.

If your enemy is an unjust person, why do you think that proof of injustice will bring about a change?

Be careful when someone suddenly becomes a lot nicer than you are.

Success may not mean you did right.

Wherever you live, town or country, a command as cruel as a tiger paw fastens on you, and you become what the town or country says.

Pride goes before a fall, but sometimes you fall anyway.

No matter how well or loud you speak, none of the stars will stop to listen.

Whatever I break, I'll pay the damages.

Things I Learned Last Week

Ants, when they meet each other,
usually pass on the right.

Sometimes you can open a sticky
door with your elbow.

A man in Boston has dedicated himself
to telling about injustice.
For three thousand dollars he will
come to your town and tell you about it.

Schopenhauer was a pessimist but
he played the flute.

Yeats, Pound, and Eliot saw art as
growing from other art. They studied that.

If I ever die, I'd like it to be
in the evening. That way, I'll have
all the dark to go with me, and no one
will see how I begin to hobble along.

In The Pentagon one person's job is to
take pins out of towns, hills, and fields,
and then save the pins for later.

Maybe what I see is there.

The fiction is that we're all equally responsible for what our government does.

My preference for lies isn't just for my own—I like other people's lies too. History is the lies people have agreed on?

Mistake: we assume more light will reveal all that there is.

We survive by our limitations.

People look at my books on Gandhi and say, "He didn't prevail against his enemies." These people don't even consider that there might be some aim other than their idea of prevailing.

We should breathe carefully, even if no tigers live here.

Most people explore on roads already made.

We decided not to climb some of the mountains, because they were there.

All poems are found poems.

You should go wherever you go as yourself, no more, no less, exactly so. The mistakes you make should be your own, and the perceptions.

Even without faith a mountain may move.

Are some of the enemy better than others?

In a democracy, some of the assumptions require that persons be ready to follow their thoughts and win or lose. What if certain goals are much more important than others—should you practice tactics on minor issues in order to hold true on the major ones? (No. The person you face deserves the full encounter of your true self on whatever the topic is.) Read with your brights full on. Write with a glass typewriter—full disclosure throughout. Listen with sympathy. Speak like a child. Maybe *occasions* for different assumptions? Irony sometimes, contests to win. But sometimes:—all cards on the table.

Tuned In Late One Night

Listen—this is a faint station
left alive in the vast universe.
I was left here to tell you a message
designed for your instruction or comfort,
but now that my world is gone I crave
expression pure as all the space
around me: I want to tell what is. . . .

Remember?—we learned that still-face way,
to wait in election or meeting and then
to choose the side that wins, a leader
that lasted, a president that stayed in?
But some of us knew even then it was better
to lose if that was the way our chosen
side came out, in truth, at the end.

It's like this, truth is: it's looking out while everything
happens; being in a place of your own,
between your ears; and any person
you face will get the full encounter
of your self. When you hear any news
you ought to register delight or pain
depending on where you really live.

Now I am fading, with this ambition:
to read with my brights full on,
to write on a clear glass typewriter,
to listen with sympathy,
to speak like a child.

Always do your writing in the wilderness.

Lostness is a function of your assumptions about where you belong.

Harness all the sled dogs.

It is not the sound of the ax that cuts the tree.

Everyone is a conscientious objector to something.

A box arrived. It said, "Any side up."

Most people live lives that are too significant.

On the coast you have one main neighbor.

You like the moon but you wouldn't want it in your house or any bigger.

Frogs met all night but didn't settle anything.

Day, night, storms, the seasons—only these need
happen. All else is clutter.

At first it's not much of a river.

If you live by truth, any thought belongs.

Strange, the best part of a room is a window.

My belief is what my whole life says.

Acknowledgments

Grateful acknowledgments are due to the following publications where some of this book's aphorisms and poems have previously appeared:

Aphorisms

"Poetry is the kind of thing you have to see from the corner of your eye . . ." William Stafford, *Writing the Australian Crawl* (Ann Arbor: University of Michigan Press, 1978). Copyright © The Estate of William Stafford.

"Somewhere deep where we have no program . . ."; "The things you do not have to say make you rich. . . ."; "'Drink from your own well,' Kierkegaard said"; "Harness all the sled dogs." William Stafford, *Crossing Unmarked Snow: Further Views on the Writer's Vocation*, edited by Paul Merchant and Vincent Wixon. Copyright © 1998 by the University of Michigan Press.

"Just a succession of things the way the world gives you things . . . an aggregation of things to say." *William Stafford: The Life of the Poem* (Ashland, OR: TTTD Productions, 1989, video); William Stafford, *Crossing Unmarked Snow: Further Views on the Writer's Vocation*, edited by Paul Merchant and Vincent Wixon. Copyright © 1998 by the University of Michigan Press.

"Sometimes, Reading." *Ohio Review* (fall 1993); William Stafford, *Crossing Unmarked Snow: Further Views on the Writer's Vocation*, edited by Paul Merchant and Vincent Wixon. Copyright © 1998 by the University of Michigan Press.

"The Current of Humanity: Carolyn Forché's *Against Forgetting: Twentieth Century Poetry of Witness.*" *Hungry Mind Review* 28 (winter 1993–94); William Stafford, *Crossing Unmarked Snow: Further Views on the Writer's Vocation*, edited by Paul Merchant and Vincent Wixon. Copyright © 1998 by the University of Michigan Press.

"All events and experiences are local, somewhere." *Tennessee Poetry Journal* 1, no. 1 (fall 1967); reprinted in *Tennessee Poetry Journal* 4, no. 1 (fall 1970); reprinted as "On

Being Local" in *Northwest Review* 13, no. 3 (1973); reprinted (with first line as title) in the *Christian Science Monitor*, March 14, 1974; William Stafford, *Crossing Unmarked Snow: Further Views on the Writer's Vocation*, edited by Paul Merchant and Vincent Wixon. Copyright © 1998 by the University of Michigan Press.

"A poem knows where you already are . . ."; "Always do your writing in the wilderness." *Taking Note: From Poets' Notebooks*, edited by Stephen Kuusisto, Deborah Tall, and David Weiss (Geneva, NY: Hobart and William Smith Colleges Press, 1991), a special issue of *Seneca Review* 21, no. 2; reprinted in *The Poet's Notebook: Excerpts from the Notebooks of 26 American Poets*, edited by Stephen Kuusisto, Deborah Tall, and David Weiss (New York: W. W. Norton and Company, 1995); William Stafford, *Crossing Unmarked Snow: Further Views on the Writer's Vocation*, edited by Paul Merchant and Vincent Wixon. Copyright © 1998 by the University of Michigan Press.

"We are surrounded, not by emblems, by paragons or villains . . ."; "What if you could stun everyone into having the same good dream . . ."; "Poems are expendable . . ."; "Treat the world as if it really existed."; "Any chunk of carbon under pressure will turn into a diamond." William Stafford, *The Answers Are Inside the Mountains: Meditations on the Writing Life*, edited by Paul Merchant and Vincent Wixon. Copyright © 2003 by the University of Michigan Press.

"What a person is shows up in what a person does," "An Interview with William Stafford," with Michael Fallon and Anthony McGurrin, *Maryland Poetry Review* (spring–summer 1988); William Stafford, *The Answers Are Inside the Mountains*, edited by Paul Merchant and Vincent Wixon. Copyright © 2003 by the University of Michigan Press.

"Lostness is a function of your assumptions about where you belong." *William Stafford: The Life of the Poem* (Ashland, OR: TTTD Productions, 1989); William Stafford, *The Answers Are Inside the Mountains*, edited by Paul Merchant and Vincent Wixon. Copyright © 2003 by the University of Michigan Press.

"Art is first nothing, then something," "Fishing Your Life, Bonuses, and the Helicopter Arts: Interview with William Stafford," Gala Muench, *Connections* (autumn 2001);

William Stafford, *The Answers Are Inside the Mountains*, edited by Paul Merchant and Vincent Wixon. Copyright © 2003 by the University of Michigan Press.

"The grace we need to find will not be found by the graceful only." Kim Stafford, *The Muses Among Us* (Athens, GA: The University of Georgia Press, 2003).

"Language is my friend. I feel the language the same way a fish feels water." *Pacific Review* 23, no. 1 (1982). Copyright © The Estate of William Stafford.

"My attitude is this: where you live is not crucial, but how you *feel* about where you live is crucial." *At the Field's End*, edited by Nicholas O'Connell (Seattle: Madrona Publishers, 1987). Copyright © The Estate of William Stafford.

"A gun can choose. A bullet has no choice." *Taking Note: From Poets' Notebooks*, edited by Stephen Kuusisto, Deborah Tall, and David Weiss (Geneva, NY: Hobart and William Smith Colleges Press, 1991), a special issue of *Seneca Review* 21, no. 2; reprinted in *The Poet's Notebook: Excerpts from the Notebooks of 26 American Poets*, edited by Stephen Kuusisto, Deborah Tall, and David Weiss (New York: W. W. Norton and Company, 1995). Copyright © The Estate of William Stafford.

"When the snake decided to go straight, he didn't get anywhere." *Pilgrimage* 28, no. 2 (2004). Copyright © The Estate of William Stafford.

"As you know, my poems are organically grown," "Some Notes on Writing," *An Oregon Message* (New York: Harper and Row, 1987). Copyright © The Estate of William Stafford.

"Before you have your dreams . . ."; "A river that had one bank was lost."; "Where there is no directive all ways are equally good . . ."; "Oregon is insanely green . . ."; "Water is always ready to learn"; "The stream is always revising"; "If you live by truth, any thought belongs"; "The river keeps looking for the perfect stone"; "At first it's not much of a river." Cut into stones in Frank Boyden's William Stafford installation at Foothills Park on the Willamette River, Lake Oswego, Oregon, 31 August 2005. Copyright © The Estate of William Stafford.

"To hold the voice down . . ."; "What the locomotive says . . ."; "Arrows punish a bow."; "Truth has no perspective"; "My tremors are small . . ."; "You are part of what you criticize . . ."; "Beat your megaphones into ear trumpets"; "Save the world by . . ."; "My belief is . . ."; "Being wrong is easy . . ."; "Winners can lose what winning was for"; "The eye that can . . ."; "Some questions you would ask . . ."; "The root and the flower . . ."; "Other parts of the car . . ."; "A Response to Those Who Told Us . . ."; "Between roars the lion purrs"; "We survive by our limitations"; "Intentions have side effects"; "I live in a foreign country"; "You may win a war you are sorry to have started"; "Mistakes you make are guides . . ."; "The wars we haven't had saved many lives"; "On a battlefield the flies don't care who wins"; "Success may not mean you did right"; "The arrow tells what the archer meant to say"; "People look at my books on Gandhi . . ."; "Come, be human. Sit down and let's talk"; "You like the moon but . . ."; "My preference for lies . . ."; "The truth is, every day . . ."; "It's a constant struggle . . ." *Every War Has Two Losers*, edited by Kim Stafford (Minneapolis: Milkweed Press, 2003). Copyright © 2003 The Estate of William Stafford.

"When he saw the leopard jump . . ."; "Off a high place . . ."; "So light the bird . . ."; "It is legitimate to crawl . . ."; "To be happy only with unattainable things"; "Successful people are in a rut"; "Every mountain has that one place . . ."; "The cost of epics . . ."; "Lost pioneers were the ones . . ."; "Before you have your dreams . . ."; "There is such a thing as helping history . . ."; "If there is a trail . . ."; "You hope. But you know."; "My kind of faith is . . ."; "It is not the sound of the ax . . ."; "By the sound a pen makes . . ."; "The ideal teacher . . ."; "Maybe we're just worms . . ."; "Water is always ready to learn"; "The Sun is thousands of times . . ."; "You can be drowning and like it . . ."; "Why should I worry? . . ."; "Like a frog at a moonrise . . ."; "A rejection slip . . ."; "At first it's not much of a river." *In Pieces: An Anthology of Fragmentary Writing*, edited by Olivia Drescher (Seattle: Impassio Press, 2006). Copyright © The Estate of William Stafford.

"Writing must learn to be as easy as talk"; "Rocks that fail become sand"; "You are inside the story, telling it . . ."; "If we are to have great poets . . ."; "In writing, a trick is to give yourself good assignments." Printed in the Lewis &

Clark College Fifth William Stafford Symposium booklet to accompany Naomi Shihab Nye's visit, 4–5 November 2005, Portland, Oregon. Copyright © The Estate of William Stafford.

"I don't want to do anything *to be an example* to anyone."; "Aphorisms gathered as a poem: A well-oiled gate . . ." *Friends of William Stafford: A Newsletter for Poets & Poetry* 15, no. 1 (spring 2010). Copyright © The Estate of William Stafford.

"By the sound a pen makes . . ."; "Joseph Conrad and the sea . . ."; "Entering a book is letting it change you." *Friends of William Stafford: A Newsletter for Poets & Poetry* 16, no. 1 (spring 2011). Copyright © The Estate of William Stafford.

Poems

"Artist, Come Home," "*Mein Kampf.*" William Stafford, *The Way It Is: New & Selected Poems.* Copyright © 1998 Graywolf Press. Reprinted with the permission of The Permissions Company, Inc., on behalf of Graywolf Press, Minneapolis, Minnesota, www.graywolfpress.org. Reprinted in William Stafford, *Ask Me: 100 Essential Poems*, edited by Kim Stafford (St. Paul: Graywolf Press, 2014).

"Buddha's Thoughts." *Paintbrush,* October 1986. Copyright © The Estate of William Stafford.

"Butterflies in the Radiator Grill." William Stafford, *Weather* (Mt. Horeb, WI: Perishable Press, 1969). Copyright © The Estate of William Stafford.

"Climbing Along the River." William Stafford, *Learning to Live in the World,* edited by Jerry Watson and Laura Apol Obblink (New York: Harcourt, Brace and Company, 1994); William Stafford, *The Way It Is: New & Selected Poems.* Copyright © 1998 Graywolf Press. Reprinted with the permission of The Permissions Company, Inc., on behalf of Graywolf Press, Minneapolis, Minnesota, www.graywolfpress.org. Reprinted in William Stafford, *Ask Me: 100 Essential* Poems, edited by Kim Stafford (St. Paul: Graywolf Press, 2014).

"Consolations," "Salvaged Parts," "Sayings from the Northern Ice," "So Long," "Written on the Stub of the First Paycheck." William Stafford, *The Darkness Around Us Is*

Deep, edited by Robert Bly (New York: HarperCollins, 1993). William Stafford. *The Way It Is: New & Selected Poems.* Copyright © 1998 Graywolf Press. Reprinted with the permission of The Permissions Company, Inc., on behalf of Graywolf Press, Minneapolis, Minnesota, www.graywolfpress.org.

"The Dream of Now," "Keepsakes," "Note." William Stafford, *Learning to Live in the World*, edited by Jerry Watson and Laura Apol Obblink. New York: Harcourt, Brace and Company, 1994; William Stafford, *The Way It Is: New & Selected Poems*. Copyright © 1998 Graywolf Press. Reprinted with the permission of The Permissions Company, Inc., on behalf of Graywolf Press, Minneapolis, Minnesota, www.graywolfpress.org.

"The Gospel Is Whatever Happens." William Stafford, *Passwords* (New York: HarperCollins, 1991). Copyright © The Estate of William Stafford.

"Influential Writers." William Stafford, *Even in Quiet Places*. Copyright © 1996 by The Estate of William Stafford. Reprinted with the permission of The Permissions Company, Inc., on behalf of Confluence Press, www.confluencepress.com. Reprinted in *The Way It Is: New & Selected Poems*. St. Paul: Graywolf Press, 1998.

".38." William Stafford, *My Name Is William Tell*. Copyright © 1992 by William Stafford. Reprinted with the permission of The Permissions Company, Inc., on behalf of Confluence Press, www.confluencepress.com. Reprinted in William Stafford, *The Way It Is: New & Selected Poems* (St. Paul: Graywolf Press, 1998).

"Put These in Your Pipe," "Wild Horse Lore." William Stafford, *The Way It Is: New & Selected Poems*. Copyright © 1998 Graywolf Press. Reprinted with the permission of The Permissions Company, Inc., on behalf of Graywolf Press, Minneapolis, Minnesota, www.graywolfpress.org.

"Sayings of the Blind." William Stafford, *Crossing Unmarked Snow*, edited by Paul Merchant and Vincent Wixon (Ann Arbor: University of Michigan Press, 1998); William Stafford, *The Way It Is: New & Selected Poems*. Copyright © 1998 Graywolf Press. Reprinted with the permission of The Permissions Company, Inc., on behalf of Graywolf Press, Minneapolis, Minnesota, www.graywolfpress.org. Reprinted

Paul Merchant would like to express his appreciation for the responses of the following participants in a seminar on the aphorisms, "Editing William Stafford," held at the Graduate School,

Lewis & Clark College, in the fall semester, 1997: Caroline Boutard, Nora Eskes, Melanie Green, Debra Hiefield, Loretta Johnson, Joan Maiers, Debbi Monahan, Laurel Rogers, Kaia Sand, Heath Lynn Silberfeld, and Richard Turnock. Their pleasantly varied suggestions for possible editions of the aphorisms are on file at the William Stafford Archives in series 11, subseries 1, box 15, folders 1 and 2. The following interns and volunteers at the William Stafford Archives helped to create the transcripts of William Stafford's prose out of the twenty thousand pages of daily writings, from which the aphorisms were selected: Karen Bonoff, Barbara Dills, Samuel Jordan, Loretta Johnson, Abel Kloster, Diane McDevitt, Jill Teasley, and Emily Teitsworth.

This book could not have been assembled without the kind assistance of Kim Stafford, William Stafford's literary executor, and the staff at the William Stafford Archives, Lewis & Clark College, Portland, Oregon: Doug Erickson, head of Special Collections, Jeremy Skinner, Special Collections librarian, and Zach Selley, assistant archivist.